SEAHORSES

TWIG C. GEORGE

THE MILLBROOK PRESS   BROOKFIELD, CONNECTICUT

Many thanks to Jorge Gomezjurado, Senior Aquarist, Syngnathid Breeding Program, National Aquarium in Baltimore, for his work with and for seahorses and for his irreplaceable help on this book.

For Luke, Sam, Zoe, Hunter, Olivia, Jonathon, and Laura. May there always be seahorses in your world.

The seahorses on the front cover and the title page are White's seahorse, *Hippocampus Whitei*.

Published by The Millbrook Press, Inc.
2 Old New Milford Road
Brookfield, Connecticut 06804

Front cover photograph courtesy of © Jeffrey Jeffords, http://divegallery.com

Photographs courtesy of National Geographic Image Collection: pp. 1 (© George Grall), 5 (© George Grall), 23 (© George Grall), 24 (© George Grall); © Jurgen Freund / naturepl.com: p. 3; Photo Researchers, Inc: pp. 4 (© Gregory G. Dimijian, M.D.), 11 (© Daniel Heuclin), 12 (right: © Fred McConnaughey), 18 (© Gregory Ochocki), 25 (© Dr. Paul A. Zahl); © Jeffrey Jeffords, http://divegallery.com: p. 7; The National Aquarium, Baltimore: p. 8 (© George Grall); © 2003 Norbert Wu / www.norbertwu.com: pp. 10, 13, 14-15, 16-17, 30, 32; © Bert Chauvel/Visualdiving: p. 12 (left); Corbis: pp. 20 (© Stephen Frink), 26 (© Alan Towse/Ecoscene), 29 (© Kevin Fleming); © David Hall/Getty Images: p. 21; © Francesco Turano: p. 22; © Gianni Neto: p. 31.

Library of Congress Cataloging-in-Publication Data
George, Twig C.
Seahorses / Twig C. George.
p. cm.
Summary: Describes the physical characteristics, behavior, and habitats of different species of seahorses, sea dragons, and pipefish, through simple text and photographs.
ISBN 0-7613-2869-6 (lib. bdg.)
1. Sea horses—Juvenile literature. [1. Sea horses.] I. Title.
QL638.S9G46 2003   597'.6798—dc21   2003010124

Printed in the United States of America
5 4 3 2 1

Long-snouted seahorse
Hippocampus guttulatus

If you were a seahorse, you would enchant all who saw you. One glimpse of you would remind people that there was magic on Earth. You'd be that special.

Dwarf seahorse
Hippocampus zosterae

You'd also be a fish. A very unusual fish, for sure. You would float upright. Your almost invisible side fins would flutter, lightly, like eyelashes blinking.

Lined seahorse
Hippocampus erectus
and blue crab

You wouldn't use your tail fin for swimming, like other fish, because you wouldn't have one. Long ago it evolved from a fin to a monkey-like tail.

Dwarf seahorse
Hippocampus zosterae

Weedy sea dragons
Phyllopteryx taeniolatus

Without a powerful fishy sort of tail fin you wouldn't be a strong swimmer. So, you would find other ways to survive in the sea.

Instead of fighting currents, you would wrap your tail elegantly around sea grass and coral, and let the water world pass over and around you.

Pacific seahorse
Hippocampus ingens

Long-snouted seahorse
Hippocampus guttulatus

Since you couldn't speed away from your enemies, you'd hide in plain sight.

Pygmy seahorse
Hippocampus bargibanti

Spotted seahorse
Hippocampus kuda

Ornate ghostpipefish
Solenostomus paradoxus

Or, you
could curl
up among
the coral,

Spotted seahorse
Hippocampus kuda

Leafy sea dragon
Phycodurus eques

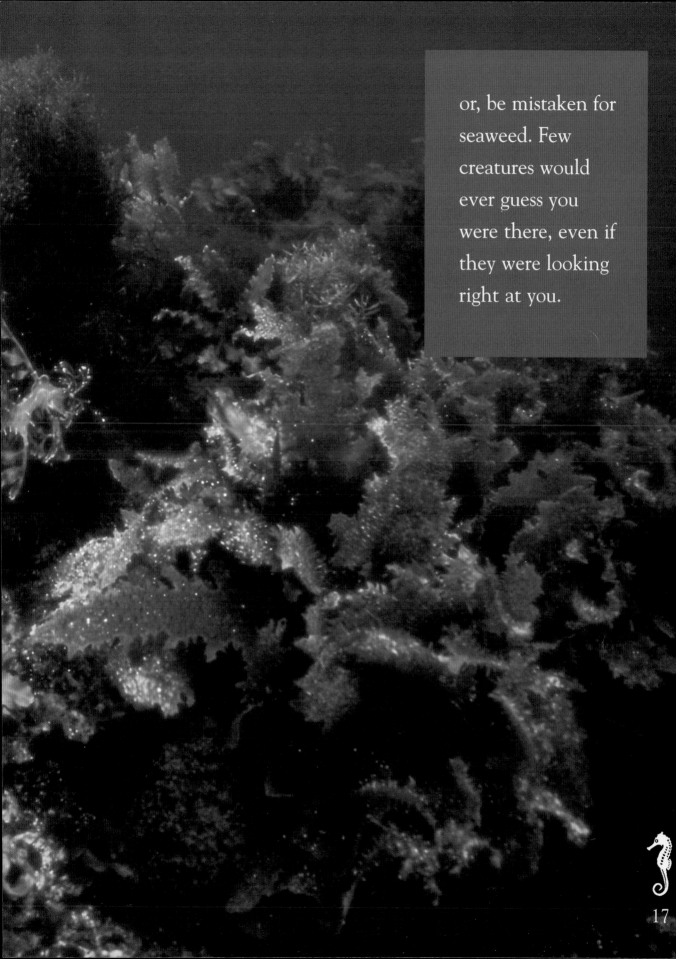

or, be mistaken for seaweed. Few creatures would ever guess you were there, even if they were looking right at you.

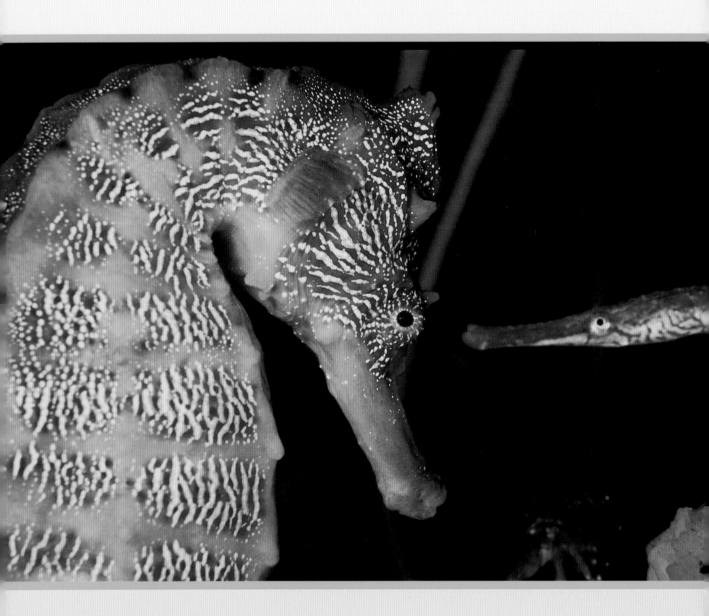

Pacific seahorse
Hippocampus ingens

Bay pipefish
Syngnathus leptorhynchus

If you were a seahorse, you could roll your eyes in two different directions, and not get dizzy. You could see where you were going and where you had come from, all at the same time. Quite a gift.

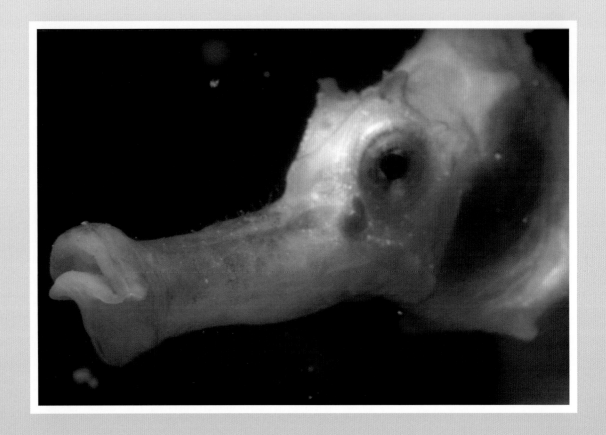

You would not have knives and forks to eat with, of course, because you wouldn't have any hands. Instead, you have gills like cheeks on each side of your head. *SNAP* you squeeze them together and force the water out. *WHOOSH* you open your gills so quickly, that you suck in everything around you with your straw-like snout. You would eat the tiniest shrimps and animals. But, if a larger fish happened to get in the way, you might suck a hunk right off him, too! In the world of seahorses being called a sucker is a compliment.

Pot-Bellied seahorse

*Hippocampus
abdominalis*

White's seahorse
giving birth
Hippocampus whitei

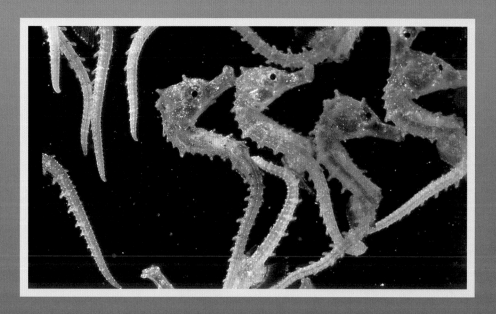

Short-headed seahorse fry
Hippocampus breviceps

If you were a seahorse father, you'd also be a
mother. A female seahorse deposits her eggs in a
male's pouch. The fathers fertilize, carry, and give
birth to thousands of babies, called fry. Hours
after the fry are launched, the fathers can become
pregnant again. That's just the way it is with
seahorses. The fry in the picture above were just born,
and in real life are about the size of this seahorse. ➜

Some fry immediately grab on to anything they can find, even their fathers. Others are pulled by the currents to grow in the open sea. Eventually, they will drift into protected places among coral and grasses and roots to live. For forty million years this has worked well for seahorses.

White's seahorse
Hippocampus whitei

Lined seahorse
Hippocampus
erectus

Dried seahorses

26

A seahorse is not a great meal. It's protected by a hard bony armor. Still penguins, tuna, stingrays, and crabs will eat them on occasion. People are a bigger problem. People take seahorses because they are beautiful. They take them because they *are* so magical. They grind them into medicines and potions, falsely believing that seahorse powder will make them stronger, or healthier, or more attractive. They dredge their grass beds, and knock over their coral. But times are changing; many people are working hard to return the seahorses to the sea, to replace the grasses and protect the coral. When one creature returns, so do others. That's magic, too.

Left alone, seahorses survive just fine in the sea. They find their tiny food. They mingle with their surroundings. They court each other and dance. Dance? Yes, dance.

When a seahorse female is ready to deposit her eggs, a male approaches her. She turns her head from side to side. Her body glimmers, changing color swiftly from brown to gold and back again. The male inflates his pouch to show her it's empty. She nods her head up and down. She accepts him. They swim belly to belly, carried by the sea and tides. They dance long and slow, every three or four days. It's a dance they will do together often. Seahorses mate for life. If one should die, the other may never find another mate that is ready to dance, at the same time, in the same way, to the same tune.

Hippocampus species
amidst plants and coral

Tiger tail seahorses
Hippocampus comes

And, what dance
would you do if you
were a seahorse?
Not just any dance.
Heads together, tails
entwined,
you would dance
the tango.

Long-snouted seahorse
hippocampus guttulatus
in front of a Featherduster worm

31

More About Seahorses, Sea Dragons, and Pipefish

Whenever I write a book like *Seahorses* I read, research, talk to experts, and go to see whatever it is I am writing about as much as possible. Then I begin. As I write, many facts get left along the way, like film clips on a cutting room floor. Some of the facts left behind I am very attached to, like the fact that some seahorses can turn a brilliant red color. Other facts are easier to leave behind. But there are always a few that I know I will get asked over and over again by my readers. So here I'm going to give you some of the facts I think you will want to know that did not find their way into the story.

The seahorse family name, *Syngnathidae*, means "fused jaws," because their mouths do not open and shut. The family includes seahorses, sea dragons, and pipefish. The smallest member of this group is the pygmy seahorse, which is about ¼ inch long full-grown. The giant Pacific seahorse can grow up to 12 inches. Sea dragons can reach 17 inches in length.

Seahorses change color and some can change their shapes by growing spines, or bumps, called cirri. These changes help them blend in with their environment.

Seahorses can be found in all the world's oceans though mainly in the warmer waters between 45 degrees north latitude to 45 degrees south latitude on the globe. The most varieties can be found in the Indo-Pacific and western Atlantic oceans.

The smaller species of seahorses may live up to one year, others three to four years, and the sea dragons are thought to live eight to ten years.

Tons of seahorses, sea dragons, and pipefish, totaling millions of individuals are taken every year. To find out more about seahorse conservation and how you can help, contact: Project Seahorse, University of British Columbia, Fisheries Centre, 2204 Main Mall, Vancouver, BC V6T 1Z4, Canada. As of this writing the web page address is http://projectseahorse.org

And, finally, what is one of my favorite facts that I had to give up? Seahorses have no teeth or stomachs. They suck in their food and digest it so quickly that some of the tiny animals they feed on come out still alive, only to be eaten again. Talk about fast food!

I hope you will find your own favorite facts as time goes on.

Enjoy!

Twig George

*Diver Jim Thiselton
and a Leafy sea dragon*